Raising Up
the Rain

Raising Up the Rain

Selected Poems

Laurie Katon

MuseStar Publishing
PRESCOTT, ARIZONA

Library of Congress Control Number: 2018902884

ISBN 978-0-692-06179-4

Artwork by Laurie Katon
Photography by Jennifer Longworth
Book design by Longworth Creative, LLC

Consulting Reader – Cheryl Berry

First Edition
Printed in the United States of America

Contents

Opening Words

We poem-makers and poem-
embracers open words
and explore the richness
they hold.
We revel in their sounds,
contemplate their meanings,
wander in the midst of
the images they evoke.

For those who are shut out,
for those who are locked in,
we wield words
that open spaces,
places to gather together.

We open with words—
we begin, and we expand.

Words shine into our minds,
igniting us with insight.

Words flow into our hearts,
imbuing us with love.

unfold
     unfurl
          reveal

these are Opening Words.

7 a.m., awakened, dazed

Seeking a vanished dream,
my mind digs in wet sand at
the ocean's edge

Polished fragments of shells
form bands that shift
with each receding wave

Ridges of foam bubble and
sink away, small holes
in the brown sand
whistle with the white sound
of underground clams

Dry kelp lies in dark streaks,
like runes that hint at the
deep's true meaning

I know what I seek is
here on this beach

or has it been dragged
back to sea
to circle in dark currents,
to rock in the surf
until flung up another evening?

Hearing Ned on the Didgeridoo

Cheeks puffed and red,
nose snorting air,
he blows into the mouth
of a long large tube.
We all stare, drums
suspended in hands,
stunned by the deep drone
that stirs the room.

The studio where we lounge
is perched on the edge
of a lush grassy slope.
Trees drip on the roof,
mist rises,
the stream rushes below.

But the air flowing out
of the didgeridoo
blows dry and hot.
Filled with the pulse
of endless sand and rock,
the sound of the earth,
the song of deep caves.
Entranced, we lift our drums
and rattle our gourds,
and our veins spiral
with aboriginal blood.

Fruitless Speculations

Fairy-tale poison apple
hiding cyanide seeds,
shiny red with razor
blades at trick or treat.

Why do we imbue
this fruit with evil?

Sweetness clamors on
the tongue, ripeness is
all we seek, and yet
there is something
at the core that
bends belief.

I have an apple slicer
that circles round the core
and cleaves six segments
neatly—my daughter won't
bite into an apple whole.

She fears for her teeth,
or else the unknown.
She'll scrutinize every
piece, and eat only
those that no rot
has reached.

If Whitman had Studied Botany

The grass is not what we see—
long green strands flowing
with waves of wind,
or blunt-edged from
shearing by machine.

What you pull up in clumps
and show me
is nothing but earth-froth
that comes forth
each spring, then dries
like wheat each fall.

The wild herds know these blades,
long trodden upon,
conceal their roots, the source
of all they need.

Underground rhizomes
that bind the land
in unseen webs
nourish the ebb
and flow above.

Flight of Ideas Takes Wing

All those who are
clumsy on the ground
or heavy on a perch,
those of hefty feathered body
who hop or hobble,
waddle or lurch on talons
or feet that are webbed

those who look like
they'll never fly—

the stars beckon, the winds urge
them on, the sky itself opens
like a vast spacious Mind

and we doubters down below
watch in awe as swans and eagles,
condors and geese, with no downward
glance, with no binding fear,
take wing, and soar and soar.

No more Daylight Savings

Four days of north winds
have purified the sky.
The clear light sweeps
fields of dry grass
and bales of hay
and trembles on
fluttering leaves.

Baroque foliage lies in
tatters on the ground,
the sky opens
around the skeletal trees,

rinsing the land in sunshine,
marking it with frail shadows.

All things seem made of reflected light
and our eyes need the long dark nights
to surround this dazzle.

Dia de los Muertos at the Rural Cemetery*

Indian summer, we call it—
though the Pequot and Mohegans are
long gone, none to be found in
this land of graves.
Nor is this where my ancestors lay,
yet I visit here among tilted headstones
and marble monuments,
mounds of brown rakings piled by
groundskeepers who bustle to
clean up autumn's leave-taking.

Canadian geese trundle toward me in
dark procession, begging for bread.
The pond glitters, as if lit by a
million tiny candles.

These are the turtles' last basking days,
as they doze on rocks jutting
amidst yellow mats of leaves.

Above the pond, a blur of wings—
dragonfly lovers circle each other,
then retreat to separate stones
where their red bodies pulse
with fading warmth.

As oak leaves twirl in silent descent,
I raise this World in offering
to the Other One.

* Day of the Dead, November 2, is a Mexican ritual graveside
celebration to commune with the spirits of deceased loved ones.

December is Deeply Shadowed

shadows tucked between
dry goldenrod stalks and
leafless bushes

shadows folded into the hollows
on the hillside
small shadows huddled behind
clumps of grass in the fields

the low sun illuminates the one
majestic oak, its massive trunk
and broad branches spotlit
in front of a dark
curtain of shadow

our own shadows keep pace
with us, extend ahead of us
on the dirt road as we
head home early
late
it is always late
in the day
in December

Strangers

You have walked past them for years,
blind to your silent neighbors.
They merge with their kin, you believe.
You don't perceive their unique ways
of seeking a bit of sun.

Finding them unmoving, your heart
is not open to the whispered sounds
that surround them, the subtle hum.
Your hand doesn't know their feel,
whether well-muscled or slim,
never touches the skin so unlike your own.
Uneasy in their terrain, you don't wander long
where they might crowd in and hide
your path home.

  Forest you roughly call them.

Know this: the soul of each oak
is in bark and bud, leaf and stem,
branches dancing in the wind.

Raising Up the Rain

The poor parched ones
among us, dwellers on dry land,
believe the rains come from above

Their eyes turn upward
and beseech the sky
for big splattering drops,
for showers or sprinkles,
thunderous torrents
or thin sheets of drizzle

But I and my soul-kin
have been granted vision
We implore the vast waters,
those that roll in the east,
those that surge in the west
We know the sea

that breathes the clouds into being
and propels the rains around the world
will, dancing with waves, receive
those rains back again
like children returning to the womb

And so we raise our voices
in prayer and incantation,
in chant and benediction
The song rises in us
from soundless depths

dust to dust
water to water
we rise, we fall
we rise, we fall

Nighttime Prayer

What more
could I pray for
when there is all this?

The distant train whistle,
my husband's breath,
the warm bed drifting
like a raft

The roots of faith
hold the earth together
Its leaves feed
the very air

Isn't that enough
of a prayer?

Divination

Hidden blessings, like portents and signs,
must be divined by those who know.

I am not trained in this art, though I
collect the hints that come to me
and display them carefully on a shelf—
the white feather of the owl,

the black one of the crow
lie next to a shiny stone;
a prickly pod from a tall weed
by a translucent insect wing.

These fragments of others' lives
come to me—like the food
I choose from the market each week.
And do I pray before my meals?
No more often than I pause and feel

each sacred object that I keep,
each gift whose giver could
teach what I need to know
to divine those blessings that flow
beneath the things we see.

Song of the Snake Spirit

Breath of night
fangs of grief
May darkened hearts
thus seek relief:

To shed the skin
of dead beliefs,
we rip the seams
of our soul

Let in the bitter medicine
and hear the healing
song unfold

Miracles

One must work a
miracle to become
a saint
but real miracles
don't take work

They flow like the
weeping of clouds
they rise like the
sap in trees

They boom like
midnight thunder
and erupt like
brimstone and lava

Miracles happen
whether we see them
or not, but
a magic show thrills
our small selves and
we'll pray for it forever.

Somnus

(for Bob)

In dark bedroom shadow
a believer, kneeling—
kneels by the faint
music of your breathing,
feels the embers that warm
your skin from within,
seeks the gentle
stirring of your limbs,
inhales the soul-scented flow
of your life's measured air.

Each breath the blessing
of this moment
for the believer,
for the sleeper.
Each breath of deep sleep
a testament of trust
in those realms
we cannot see.

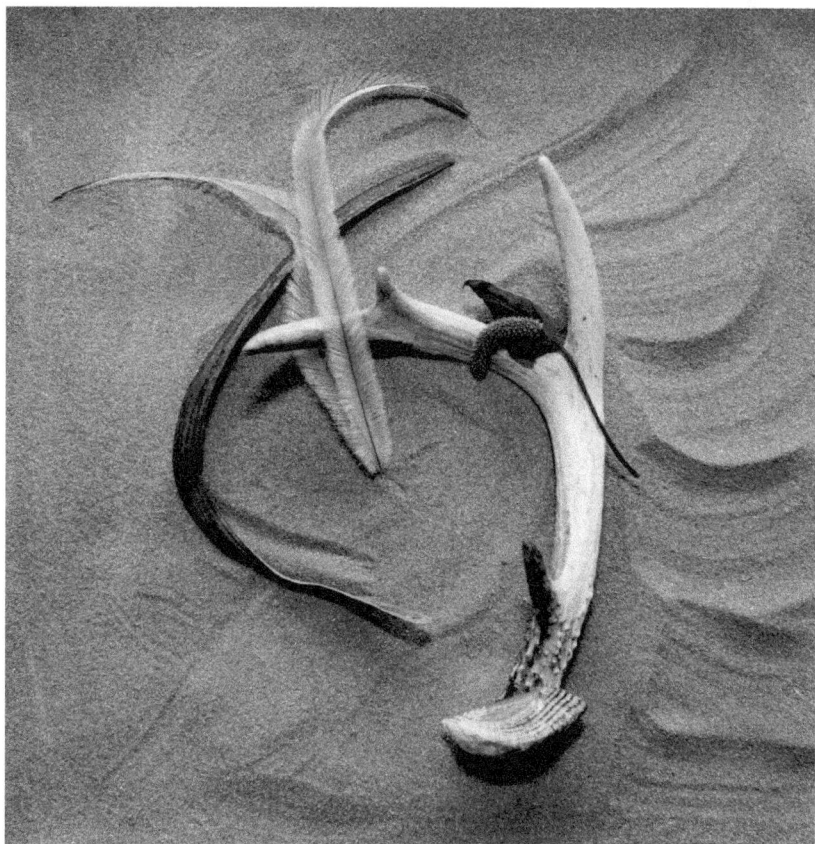

Wolves
(for Paula)

Wolf time   roaming
in the death of winter
sniffing through snow
for tracks, for shriveled
berries and scraped bark

droppings and leavings
have sustained the pack
the new moon hears
their silent howls
muffled in the throat
of memory

this is the no-bones time,
the bare den time, the
smoky dawn

yet wolf spring,
nestled in its
cocoon of fur,
sifts through skeins
of matter, seeking
to form from wild ideas
a new flesh, a hope

Seed

No air seeps into
this dark place
where a shriveled body
lies in a hard brown case

Buried in the cold earth,
deep in winter's womb,
an age-old passage
is soon to begin

The hidden life within
feels the warmth
of the unseen sun
The shell cracks,
a small white root
stirs damp dirt,

a green shoot reaches
as tiny leaves unfurl
and the guise of death
is undone

"Death and vegetables"
(for Barbara)

Summer porch, deepening dusk,
she tells me about the
mortician she met—he helps
families find another way.
He said, "It takes three days for
the body to become hollow, ready
to be laid to rest."

My friend wants to be wrapped
in soft linens, a tree planted
over her. I think of my father, very
old, his mind dissolving. I want
to touch what's left of him when the
breath departs, not just a pine box.

On her way out, I hand my friend
a bag of organic vegetables:
pale cabbage with leaves tightly
wrapped, dark beets redolent
of earth, the white bulbs of
fennel—she's got a new way
to cook the roots.

Seed of Death

Born inside the core
of each green seed,
between cells that
swell with water
and sun, is an abyss,
a speck unseen

A shadow seed
draws in all
the other does not

Leguminous,
its subtle tendrils
intertwine with
the green vines,
filling them with
the sap of time

Metamorphical

in this world of embodiment, nothing is untouched

the rain pours into field and lake alike
the chill air soaks rough stone and fern
untold millions of yearning hands
feel the shapes of beings
clothed or bare

in this world of rhythms, nothing is unmoved

the sea surge, the snail slide,
those who sway, gallop or swoop
so too do our machines move
and pulse, energy riding
the electric paths of our designing

in this world that engulfs, all is mingled

creatures partake of others,
nourished by bodies of fruit
or flesh, in a procession
of intimate encounters

in this world of fire, air, water and clay,
all lies between us

by breath inflamed,
each flows into each
dark substance and inner glow

and so we move and move
in sensuous celebration,
our minds blind,
our bodies reaching towards this
one dazzling metaphor

The Long Haul
(for a sick child)

The air is graced with dry leaves and crows.
    let go   blow free
wails the wind
as it hurtles past an empty hornets' nest.

Hope sticks like a burr.
Working it loose will loosen
a silent hemorrhage.

Dead leaves entombed in snow
will nurture earth
when spring releases them,
while rivulets of melted snow
will float a host of burrs.

The long haul is not broken,
it rises and moves even when mired in mud.

My heart has lost its rhythm—it falters and bumps.

I pray at the kitchen table
I pray at the bathroom sink

I take refuge in the buoyant
I take refuge in the dormant
I take refuge in the simple.

Mood Swings

In the eerie lime
light, patches of dead
brown moss mark the site
of the old swing set.
Where green metal poles
once sat in concrete boots,
there's no green grass yet.

Did she truly outgrow that
strange duet—my pushing
and her soaring, my stepping
back and her free fall?

Now, fevered to grow free,
she ruefully reports, "The
doctor says I'm too high"

so again I push her
to take the pills
that will bring her feet
back down to this scarred
backyard, or to her own
new ground.

Summer of the Eating Disorder

As the moon waned
and the sea drew back,
the grass turned brown
from lack of rain

All she ate was
milk and crackers,
the milk low-fat,
the crackers whole-grain

Like a prisoner who, for
an unnamed crime,
is sentenced to pay in
pounds of flesh

her body changed—
for love, for hate,
for a size-4 sexy
little dress

Her body changed
instead of her fate,
by love, by hate,
by food oppressed

Hooked on Hope

Your ex-boyfriend is still
smoking dope, I know

but you told me,
one month and three days
ago, that you had quit

I needed to hear that
and I still want to believe
it, despite the hints dropped
like dirty socks—

the bounced check
and a mention of being in
his neighborhood
(where you have no good
business to be)

But you can't
walk away from him
You take one or two steps
but you never make it to twelve

It must hurt to be so hooked

Well, I should know—
how could I
survive
without hope?

The Cell Phone of the Prodigal Daughter

She sleeps with it
she loses it at a bar
orders a new one and
asks me to accept
delivery It arrives COD
needs to be charged
I try to enjoy the music
while my party is reached

She parties too much
loses it again
I ask her to call me
when she has no phone
to let me know
it's gone   She mocks
me for clinging to my land
line, but she knows where
to find my voice
always back here at home

The Long Haul Revisited

These nine years
the long haul has
been harder and longer
than I had ever known

The stony path, the
muddy ruts, occasional smooth
going, but mostly bumpy
and long, too long

And I am not saying
this is a crossroads,
but when I look up, my
forehead is furrowed, my
shoulders ache, and despite
all the praying, my heart
is like a rock in the road

and I am thinking,
with dread and yearning,
of the road finally
diverging and of
you
pulling your own weight
on a way
of your own

No Place like ... the end of November

Watching *The Wizard of Oz*
in the dayroom at the nursing home,
I wish we three could accompany
Dorothy.

My mother, daily visitor, with her rusty
arteries recently plumbed,
she would like a new heart.

My father, straw-headed, smiles
vacantly in the wheelchair—stares
out as the thankless skies pour rain
onto black trees;
and he, who can't remember
the name for "salt", asks
Is *Desolate* a good word?

Yes it is, I say—
and I, with leonine voice,
cry out for the courage
to keep following this road
home.

Last Nap at the Old House

She sleeps almost all the time now,
nurses wake her for pills and meals.
Whenever I call, her voice is blurred,
her mind yawns and her thoughts
are dulled.

I take her on a long car ride,
just days before the house is sold.
The old furniture of the declining
years rests in place, abandoned here.

She leans her cane by the door
and totters to her bedroom,
checking dresser drawers once more
for anything left behind.

Then she lies down and naps,
head tilted, mouth open,
hand reaching
for the cat no longer there.

I wait, melancholy, in the small backyard
on a rusty lawn chair.
But when awakened
and steered out the front door,
she sheds no tear.

Agave (Century Plant)

Of my mother, they said
even as she was dying
she blossomed

She had endured most of a century,
slowly thickening flesh and juice
She had hosted many, offering
a home within herself

Memories of her own mother
were dim, hidden within
seeds-to-be

Always there was sun,
beloved sun and
fragrant showers
and once a muddy flood
that almost tore her
roots loose

And through it all, she grew
more unique, and this she
unknowingly bequeathed to me—
a tall stalk festooned with
flowers, like a spire rising
royally

April 1, 2005

(for Mom)

The mothers are dying
One by one they fall and shrivel
one by one they shrivel
and fall, some too late
and some too soon,
some too old and some
too young
I wake with dread—has her
journey ended?

As I travel to where she
fell ill, the road is
watched by red-tailed hawks,
hunched in wait
on bare limbs

On her last day,
passing that way again,
the hawks swoop and
plunge, and stoop over
prey to guard it from
vultures who hang like
kites, black nightmares
in the rising air

On that Fool's morning
as we change
the time to make room
for more light, Time
itself parts and she
passes through—thus

her eyelids look like
pale beech leaves,
battered by rains
and crushed by snows,
bleached to translucence
by the sun, like leaves so
matted to the earth they will
never be peeled away again

Just so do her eyelids lie,
closed to this life,
and I know she is
gone for good,
for better or worse,
gone from me,
from me to death

Changes

I am moving—I
tell all that I'm
ready for
a change

yes, I am worn,
my bones thinner,
waiting for light
to shine through

Yet I am not ready,
my feet unsteady

The day of my last hike to
Peters Stream, my camera
seeks plump green moss,
a gold-bottomed pool,
rushing rivulets and
rocks water-smoothed

I am not looking
to slip and fall, to be
broken and laid flat on
a rough granite slope

I have been repaired,
my bones cut and shifted
and bolted back together,
my body changed forever

Somewhere deeper
than those bones,
I know erosion,
somewhere deeper,
quakes

Brittle

Our children
            our parents
our children's parents

This birthday my arm
is in a cast, my wrist
split, stitched together
with metal pins

My daughter gives me
gifts she wants—
skin rejuvenators
and foot massagers

When the doctor
removes the staples
I have a monstrous scar

He says I'll heal
"just fine" but I
feel different

My wrist has been
replaced
with my mother's—
thin, brittle, arthritic

Our parents
            our children
our parents' children

Breakthrough

"Push yourself", my teacher says

not a gentle process

3:30 am—my mind flops
like a fish on a dock

Resignation, like a seagull cry,
pierces the fog

I am stranded, waiting
for a chance tide to
break through

Push your self

From microscopic membranes
to rough hairy hides,
each creature guards
its skin as its life

I seek a way out
through a childish pastime,
blowing bubbles:
some cease with a glistening pop,
others whirl their thin film
until they merge with sky

Renewing Buddhist Vows

To vow, to allow a part of me
the illusion that there is a
captain to this rowdy troupe
of urges, needs, beliefs and
feelings that masquerades
as a solid solo being

Creations are numberless, I vow to free them

A ladybug crawls on the zendo floor,
flees my bowing knees and praying hands,
lifts herself on shiny wings and
heads for the windowpane

Delusions are inexhaustible, I vow to abandon them

Cold floor chills my feet as I stand
and chant, variations on
I am I am I am

Reality is boundless, I vow to perceive it

A square of sunlight moves
imperceptibly up the white
wall as we slowly walk
in line, hands clasped at our chests

*The Enlightened Way is unsurpassable,
I vow to embody it*

Legs that ache from sitting folded,
cheek that itches, eyes that blink,
brain that thinks of mindless matters,
hands held palms up, serene;

breath yes breath that breathes me
to the beat of the heart (not my heart, The Heart)
the Heart of Wisdom's Perfection

Zendo Floor

Sitting in silent meditation
with eyes half-closed
I gaze at the floor-boards
of polished white oak
and suddenly see
whose bodies I walk upon—
here and at home—
whose living core has been
sacrificed with no ceremony
at lumberyard or building site

and I weep.
My teacher says these tears
speak of compassion, but
I know they hold fury too—
and yet I love the look
of shaped wood; I respect
the tools that turn it
to our use
and I know no prayers great
enough to atone
or to offer
gratitude.

Camping in Anza Borrego

Rough granite still cool
from the desert night's chill
This dirt at boulder's feet
not damp, untrodden by
scorpions and ants

I crouch and lean back here
and breathe the searing air
Already the sun turns its daunting
glare on scrabbly ground,
prickly spines and shimmering peaks

All who live here seek
the dark's mercy, and
burrow away the day
But we visitors want to hike,
to see this silent place when our
eyes insist we may
And so, blinking, unfeeling,
we stumble from shadow
to shade, and at night
we sleep the desert's
dark life away.

Avian Drama

Crows, like slivers of night,
whip through the bright April air

As breezes weave among hemlocks,
they flicker past oaks still bare

The harsh cries of the crow-mob
have driven the hawk to hide

I sit on the porch and
peer at the woods, longing
to see with raptor eyes

Sante Fe Adobe

Smooth whitewashed walls,
the roundness where
they meet the floor.
No square corners.
Each window set so deep
we can see the walls
a foot thick.

Made of straw and dirt,
adobe looks like it
could crumble into
the land where it rose.
Our yard holds a
beehive oven, once used
to bake brown loaves.

From our earth house, we drive
over Lukachukai Mountain
on an old rutted track.
In the Canyon of the Ancients
we peer at pueblo ruins,

then head back. In this time
of rains, our house still stands.
Never could a home of bricks,
wood or wallboard feel
as good as this space
within dried mud.

Autumnal Anniversary
"the air is graced with dry leaves and crows"

These crows are not
the old crows,
not last fall's crows.
These crows fly
without fury.
In a black flurry they
blow over stubbled
fields, hover
above bare trees,
mark the crisp blue
sky with wings of
gleaming purpose—

these are ravens,
I suppose,
not
crows.

Desert Mania

The days filled
with light and wind
I almost bounce.
Like gazing at a candle,
my eyes entranced—
a thin veneer of bright
sky and unrelenting
sun that has begun
to bake me into reddish stone.

Yet late at night
clouds of doubt,
like desert dust devils,
arise, whirl around
my home, the earth,
and in my dreams
dark scorpions emerge.

www.ingramcontent.com/pod-product-compliance
Lightning Source LLC
Chambersburg PA
CBHW021935040426
42448CB00008B/1078